WE DO NOT LIVE IN VAIN

SELVA CASAL

WE DO NOT LIVE IN VAIN

TRANSLATED BY
JEANNINE MARIE PITAS

velizbooks.com

Veliz Books' titles are available to the trade through our website and our
primary distributor, Small Press Distribution (800) 869.7553.
For personal orders, catalogs, or other information, write to
info@velizbooks.com

For further information write Veliz Books:
P.O. Box 961273, El Paso, TX 79996
velizbooks.com

ISBN: 978-1-949776-07-2

WE DO NOT LIVE IN VAIN

CONTENTS

SE TRATA DE UNA CASA DE AGUA

Se trata de una casa de agua
de un movimiento
un ala
como un extraño génesis
piel adentro
muerte adentro
alegría de agua
despierta la sangre macerada
felicidad del agua
labios líquidos
duro estremecimiento
abrazo espuma
cristales de la piel
vuelan los ojos húmedos
los pies se arremolinan
giran sobre sus sueños
de pronto un cementerio
un hombre a la deriva pide auxilio
avanza hasta tocar mis muertos
flota extraño agridulce
un sudor silencioso le cubre de rocío
esto que es sólo así tiene tu nombre
soles de sal y azufre
mediodías
quiero morir ahora bajo esta lluvia intemporal y clara
bajo esta ardiente certidumbre
no levantan los párpados
el duro tiempo opaco
mi corazón se ahoga en ojos clausurados
y no te veo

IT'S ABOUT A HOUSE MADE OF WATER

It's about a house made of water
a movement
a wing
like a strange genesis
skin inside
death inside
joy of water
awakens tender blood
happiness of water
liquid lips
harsh trembling
an embrace some foam
crystals of skin
humid eyes fly
feet swirl
spin over their dreams
suddenly a cemetery
a drifting man cries for help
he approaches until he touches my dead
floats strangely bittersweetly
a silent sweat covers him with dew
this which is only like this bears your name
suns of salt and sulfur
noons
I want to die right now under this timeless and clear rain
under this burning certainty
they don't lift their eyelids
harsh opaque time
my heart drowns in shut down eyes
and I don't see you

volverás de la ola
allí nos conocíamos
después
llegaron ángeles muertes
después fueron mis pies secretos
cómo decirlo ahora
océano de nuestros cuerpos hondos
los moluscos resbalan
más simples cada instante
más desnudos
perfectos derrotados
para que nada sea sino el agua
y no transcurra nadie salvo el viento.

you'll return from the wave
where we got to know each other
later
angels deaths arrived
and then came my secret feet
how do I say this now
oceans of our deep bodies
the mollusks slide
at every moment simpler
more naked
more perfected defeated
so that nothing remains but the water
and no one passes by but the wind.

HOY SE ME CAEN LOS OJOS FUSILADOS

A Pablo

Hoy se me caen los ojos fusilados
con tres gendarmes enfrente de mi puerta
adentro de mi patria
el amor es un golpe
la juventud una llaga
mi alegría
cómo decirte esto
cómo decirte nada
¡ah! no sabes qué vértigo
ayer cuando te amaba
vi un hombre en la penumbra descarnada
dientes fósiles lunas
suicidas que lloraban
yo te escribo esta carta
y se desploma el mundo
yo no sé si hemos muerto
con qué labios
con qué luz nos rozamos
si hay tiempo en nuestras horas
somos 1972 un vértigo
deja que el cielo caiga
que a las 3 que a las 4
este país se incendie de horribles pesadillas
que corran hombres grises por las calles
nos habían enseñado la dulzura
nos habían enseñado a concurrir al hombre
mas a veces tiene razón la muerte
este día distinto
esta tarde de fiebre

TODAY MY EYES FALL, SHOT BY GUNS

To Pablo

Today my eyes fall, shot by guns
with three police officers at my door
in my country
love is a blow
youth is a wound
my joy
how to tell you this
how to say nothing
ah! you don't know the vertigo
yesterday while loving you
I saw a man in the grim half-light
teeth fossils moons
weeping suicides
I'm writing you this letter
and the world is collapsing
I don't even know if we've died
what lips
what light we spend our time with
if there's even any time in our hours
we are 1972 a vertigo
so let the sky fall
so at 3 so at 4
this country might blaze with horrible nightmares
let grey men run through the streets
they had taught us tenderness
they had taught us to get along with others
but sometimes death is correct
on this distinctive day
this feverish afternoon

quise ver esa gente
ese mar
esa llaga
por la espalda
con los brazos en alto asesinados
yo me afilio a este mundo
a las bocas que crecen
a los muertos que andan
¡ah! no sabes
ya no mueren callados
ya salen a la calle
ya arremeten
necesitan de la mujer y el vientre
necesitan del hombre
en las flores de mi pared no había esto
esto digo sangre
hombres atravesados de metralla
gente y furia
porque yo venía de un país sin muerte.

I tried to see those people
that sea
those wounds
on their backs
with arms lifted murdered
I belong to this world
to the mouths that grow
to the dead that walk
oh! you don't know
they no longer die silently
now they go into the street
now they strike
they need the woman and her womb
they need the man
in the flowers of my wall there was none of this
I mean this blood
men pierced by shrapnel
people and rage
because I came from a land with no death.

QUIERO EL MAR EN LA ALCOBA

Quiero el mar en la alcoba
su resaca su ausencia
desde esta telaraña donde vivo
respiro tus secretos
no cierren no mis ojos
sigan golpeándome
madre estaba absurda
aquella tarde en que nací
sabiéndote a madre
ahora es como tu ausencia la vida
y el amor un inmenso naufragio
donde nadie recuerda
tú querías que yo fuera así
pero aún es más hondo mi quehacer
consiste en descubrir paredes
volar desde los pájaros del amanecer
esperar abrazar
caer en un campo de sangre y de batalla
la batalla es mi pelo y mi arrebato
me arrojo por las calles
corro vuelo
no sé qué cosa me hace ser así
que siempre van al mar
gritando hombre desafiando hombre masticando hombre
me escondo en los cafés y escucho
me despierto y escucho
como al descuido
todo penetra por mis dedos
las casas temblorosas
las banderas

I WANT THE SEA IN MY ROOM

I want the sea in my room
its undertow its absence
from this spiderweb I live in
I breathe your secrets
I tell my eyes don't close please don't
keep on hitting me
mother was absurd
that afternoon when I was born
and tasted you as mother
now life is like your absence
and love an immense shipwreck
where no one remembers
you wanted me to be like this
but my task is even deeper
it requires me to discover walls
to fly from daybreak's birds
to hope to embrace
to land on a field of blood and battle
the battle is my hair and my rage
I throw myself through the streets
I run I fly
I don't know what makes me this way
they always go to the sea
shouting man defying man chewing man
I hide in cafés and listen
I wake up and listen
as if carelessly
everything penetrates my fingers
the trembling houses
the flags

los domésticos días
y aquellos otros punzantes solos
expuestos al silencio
como éste
no me hieras ya más que estoy desnuda
está tu rostro adentro
está tu vida adentro
yo no sé cómo eras cómo andabas
qué piezas descubrías
hoy baja tu mirada de un ómnibus secreto
expande tu mirada el mundo
mi corázon se hiela
estarás a la puerta de la noche esperando
estarás en la boca de la nada
esperándome
como un suicido que quiere retornar
como un oleaje
un astro desaparecido
que no consta en las sombras
en los anales de este dios terrible
no es juego es llama
es que no sé morirme de otra forma
respirar de otra forma
esta luz
esta ruina donde duermo y despierto
que nadie toque tus huesos
que nadie arda detrás de tu camisa
que no mueran las llaves en que habitas
desconocida calle
noche definitiva
es el mar
es el mar
cada ola nos revive y nos mata

the household days
and those other ones piercing alone
exposed to the silence
like this one
don't hurt me especially now that I'm naked
your face is inside
your life is inside
I don't know what you were like how you moved
what rooms you discovered
today your gaze gets off a secret bus
your gaze expands the world
my heart freezes
you'll be at night's door waiting
you'll be in the mouth of nothingness
waiting for me
like a suicide who wants to come back
like a swell of waves
a vanished star
that's not recorded in the shadows
in the annals of this terrible god
it's not a game it's a flame
it's that I don't know how to die any other way
to breathe any other way
this light
this ruin where I sleep and awaken
may no one touch your bones
may no one burn behind your shirt
may the keys you dwell in not die
unknown street
definitive night
it's the sea
it's the sea
each wave revives and kills us

es un reloj de noche y en silencio
es una almohada rota
es esta vida absurda
donde cesan amantes y quehaceres
nunca me dejes sola
ni aun muerta no me dejes
estoy golpeando siempre
deja que los fusiles penetren en la alcoba
como en cruenta batalla
que entre el mar en la alcoba
mira
espuma en las paredes
caracolas
de noche y caminando
la noche nos devora
no me arrojes así que no hay ventanas
tuyas son las arañas y el absurdo
viento desconectado
un hongo inmenso nace de las bocas que aman
como entre los escombros resucito
sólo he sido por esto
he construido casas escaleras
engendrado mil hijos
apuñalado hombres
despierto entre montañas de cuerpos y te busco
busco tu forma exacta
el duro origen donde está tu nombre.

it's a clock at night in silence
it's a broken pillow
it's this absurd life
where lovers and chores cease
never leave me alone
even when I'm dead don't leave me
I'm always knocking
let the guns penetrate the room
as in bloody battle
let the sea come into the room
look
foam on the walls
seashells of the night
seashells walking
night devours us
don't throw me since there are no windows
yours are the spiders and the absurd
disjointed wind
an immense mushroom rises from loving mouths
as I rise again amid rubble
I have only existed for this
I've built houses stairwells
given birth to a thousand children
stabbed men
I awaken amid mountains of bodies and seek you
I seek your exact shape
the harsh origin that bears your name.

AMOR ESCUCHA LAS SIRENAS

Amor escucha las sirenas
cómo gritan y entran por las puertas y casas
cómo llaman
dicen que estamos solos arrojados al aire
destruidos.
Vivir es peligroso.
Escucha cómo llaman
cómo gritan y aúllan las sirenas.

LISTEN TO THE SIRENS MY LOVE

Listen to the sirens my love
how they shout and come in through the doors and houses
how they call
they say we're alone thrown out to the air
destroyed.
Living is dangerous.
Listen to the sirens
how they call they shout they howl.

YA NO HAY MAR

Ya no hay mar
hay balas
vuelves de la ola y avanzas
silba la bala silba
en la espuma dorada
espuma sangre mar
hoy un hombre absurdo crece
dentro de tus ojos
no tiene mar ni casa
es el mundo cotidiano
violento hasta el delirio
que te toma los pies y te arrebata
que te sube los pies
y te devora
te extiende desnudo y solo
sobre la muerte
como sobre un paisaje de mentira
ya no hay mar
hay balas
hay este mundo diplomado en sangre
desfiles agresiones
después
asumen voces estadísticas
y dicen sistema democrático.

THERE'S NO SEA ANYMORE

There's no sea anymore
there are bullets
you come back from the wave and move forward
the bullet hisses it hisses
on the golden foam
foam blood sea
today an absurd man is growing
in your eyes
he has neither sea nor house
he's the everyday world
violent to the point of delirium
that grabs you by the feet and snatches you
climbs up your feet
and devours you
lays you out naked and alone
over death
as over a landscape of lies
there's no sea anymore
there are bullets
there's this world licensed in blood
parades assaults
later
they put on statisticians' voices
and say democratic system.

VIENTO DE NUESTRA NOCHE

Viento de nuestra noche
duro viento
yo soy el viento amor
yo soy el viento
dejo mi cuerpo en una vida extraña
dejo mi cuerpo y vuelvo
esta tarde yo vi un hombre en la calle
desplomado vacío
era mi propia muerte
desprendida de mí
adelantada
llego con llaves y con puertas
yo soy el viento amor todo lo dejo
aliento rechinar de ventanas
ojos que ven el mundo
que tú tocas y sueñas
no llevan mi esqueleto
que se llevan el viento
aire que vuela y mata
remolino
con balas y con sangre
cae el mundo en tu cuerpo
yo lo veo lo siento
nadie duerme en la piel
en nuestro abrazo penetran los fusiles
la noche
un extraño estertor de bocas y cuchillos
quiero sus calles quiero sus secretos
ésta es la noche y mira
no estamos solos nunca

WIND OF OUR NIGHT

Wind of our night
harsh wind
I am the wind dear
I am the wind
I leave my body in a strange life
I leave my body and return
this afternoon I saw a man in the street
collapsed empty
it was my own death
detached from me
ahead of me
I show up with keys and doors
I am the wind my dear I leave it all behind
a breath a creaking of windows
eyes seeing the world
that you touch and dream
they don't carry my skeleton
they carry off the wind
air that flies and kills
a whirlwind
with bullets and blood
the world collapses into your body
I see it I feel it
no one sleeps in our skin
guns penetrate our embrace
the night
a strange death rattle of mouths and knives
I want its streets I want its secrets
this is the night and it's watching
we are never alone

mueren aúllan dentro de nuestro vértigo
gritan sol gritan hombre
toca mi cuerpo
siente por fin que no soy yo
que soy ellos
mirándote doliéndote.

they die they howl in our vertigo
they cry for sun they cry for man
touch my body
feel at last I am not myself
I am them
watching you wounding you.

NOSOTROS SOMOS FANTASMAS

Nosotros somos fantasmas que tocamos la noche
nosotros somos fantasmas
alguien está herido llama
tiemblo como un pájaro
apretado en un puño
como un niño
es de noche y golpean están asesinando a un hombre
en algún lugar
alguien desprendido de su cuerpo
me mira me ama me toca
siento ruido de lápices de sillas de ventanas
puede entrar
ahora en mi cama en este cuarto
yo quiero vivir en ti
como un glóbulo rojo en la corriente de la sangre
yo quiero vivir en ti
como un diente una mano
un pensamiento
me dejas sin saber que en la noche caigo entera
como un cuerpo que cae y cae
es de noche y entra con un cuchillo
se oyen los gritos de un hombre torturado
están torturando a un hombre
es de noche y parece que dormimos
una figura se esconde entre las ropas
un gato salta por la ventana y es mentira
los zapatos recuerdan que eran felices
es de noche un cuerpo cae a fondo.

WE ARE GHOSTS

We are ghosts that graze the night
we are ghosts
someone is wounded someone calls out
I tremble like a bird
clasped in a fist
like a child
it's night and they're knocking they're killing a man
somewhere
someone detached from their body
looks at me loves me touches me
I hear the sound of pencils chairs windows
it comes in
now in my bed in this room
I want to live within you
like a red globule in the current of blood
I want to live within you
like a tooth a hand
a thought
you leave me without knowing that at night I fall completely
like a body that falls and falls
it's night and they come in with a knife
I hear the screams of a tortured man
they are torturing a man
it's night and it seems we're asleep
a figure is hiding among the clothes
a cat jumps through the window but it's a lie
the shoes remember they were happy
it's night a body is falling deeply.

ESTOY SOLA EN LA NOCHE

Estoy sola en la noche
despierto a este conjuro
seguro y obstinado como la muerte
que persiste que golpea
nos hace padecer sonreír
un día cuando estés muerto
olvidado de todo
este amor
una hermosa noche de verano
irá a resucitarte
y resucitarán las hojas todas
y tú estarás como te dé la gana
tomando un vaso y otro
y una noche y otra
un día cuando estés lejos
mirando el mar que estaba allí
los reyes y los presidentes que desfilan
escuchando los gritos de los ahogados
de los recién nacidos
y todo lo terrible que hay en los rincones
cuando caen los zapatos
y te golpeo y te golpeo
cuando resuene en tu memoria el mundo
lanzando alaridos como una bestia herida
este amor sin nadie solo
sin hacer nada
sin decir nada
aunque nos miremos sin reconocernos
estará allí donde estuviste
donde estés
irá a buscarte.

I'M ALONE IN THE NIGHT

I'm alone in the night
awake at this incantation
as certain and stubborn as death
which persists which strikes
makes us suffer smile
one day when you're dead
when you've forgotten it all
this love
a gorgeous summer night
will come to raise you up
and all the leaves will be raised
and you'll do whatever you want
drinking glass after glass
night after night
one day when you're far away
looking at the sea that was there
the parade of kings and presidents
hearing the cries of the drowned
of the newly born
and the terrible truths in the corners
when shoes fall
and I strike you again and again
when the world resounds in your memory
shrieking like a wounded beast
this love alone on its own
doing nothing
saying nothing
though we don't recognize each other
it will be in the place where you were
where you are
and come looking for you.

A VECES UNA TERRIBLE OSCURIDAD

A veces una terrible oscuridad llena tu rostro
tus palabras
me estremecen hasta las lágrimas
y pregunto por qué entonces
tanto estupor
qué somos
quisiera encontrarme contigo
en un país de diez mil ojos
donde nadie supiera quién es
qué significa
y fuéramos tan felices como ahora
sin ahora
y nunca más pudieras evocar en mí
la aflicción de los lápices oficinas concursos
ni me interrogaras de qué casa vengo
ni a quien amé
porque súbitamente me asombran las palabras
y el terror de caer
de perder la demencia
la alegría
quisiera que enriquecidos de insectos y de pájaros
recorriéramos una isla infinita
que me hablaras de ventanas de perros
de asuntos imposibles que nadie aprobará
y jamás me recordaras ciudadanos respetables
los hondos animales y las flores
no nacen de códigos
quisiera que arrancaras nuestros corazones
y los lanzaras a la ola más alta
que fuéramos anónimos
y que arrebatados de piedad
juntos cometiéramos grandes desatinos.

SOMETIMES A TERRIBLE DARKNESS

Sometimes a terrible darkness fills your face
your words
make me tremble to the point of tears
and I ask why then
such stupor
what are we
I'd like to find myself with you
in a country of ten thousand eyes
where no one knows who they are
what they mean
and we'd be as happy as we are now
without now
and never again could you evoke in me
the affliction of pencils offices contests
you'd never ask me what house I come from
or whom I loved
because suddenly those words astound me
and the terror of falling
of losing my insanity
my joy
I'd like us enriched with insects and birds
to traverse an infinite island
and for you to speak to me of dogs of windows
of impossible matters no one will accept
and you'll never remind me of respectable citizens
the profound animals and the flowers
aren't born from codes
I'd like you to tear out our hearts
and throw them to the highest wave
let us become anonymous
so that seized by mercy
together we'll make marvelous mistakes.

LOS TELÉFONOS SUENAN

Los teléfonos suenan
solos contra la noche
solos contra la nada
no oigo
estoy dormida
muerta
andas por las paredes los espejos
te invento y tú me matas
arde un ángel
nos devora el absurdo
¡ah! si pudiera
extraños los hermanos
ciego el tiempo
entre mis sombras y entre mis afanes
hoy sólo a ti te amo
golpeas dueles
porque yo quiero llueve
yo no sé que nos pasa
de nuevo este silencio
desconectado y solo
perdido entre cabellos inventarios
irrumpo en una pieza desolada
sueño
una lámpara muerde mis entrañas
los teléfonos suenan
solos contra la noche
solos contra la nada
nadie responde nunca
nadie despierta.

THE TELEPHONES ARE RINGING

The telephones are ringing
alone against the night
alone against nothingness
I don't hear them
I'm asleep
dead
you walk among the walls the mirrors
I invent you and you kill me
an angel burns
the absurd devours us
oh! if only I could
the brothers are strange
time is blind
among my shadows and among my desires
today I love only you
you strike you hurt
it rains because I desire it
I don't know what's happening to us
again this silence
disconnected and alone
lost among hairs inventories
I break into a desolate room
I dream
a lamp bites my insides
the telephones are ringing
alone against the night
alone against nothingness
no one ever answers
no one wakes up.

COMO UN NAUFRAGIO

Como un naufragio
una serie televisada
un programa visto y vuelto a ver
como una silla
como un perro a medianoche
como que me estás quitando la piel
y la piel es infinita
estamos solos
los brazos las uñas el vacío
para morir me arrojaría al mar
para morir me arrojaría al aire
me cubriría toda
de tierra densa y oscura
yo no podría morir
no estoy conmigo no
ando sobre la sombra de otra vida
cuelgo de los andamios y los yunques
me vuelvo lumbre vegetal hierro
de madrugada a veces me levanto
a escuchar las sirenas de su voz
su día proletario
adiós gracias al cuerpo
a la mirada
sólo el golpe la espuma
sólo la desnudez me reconforta
yo soy la tierra y me deshago
entro por las ventanas
llamo a las puertas de las casas
veo correr la sangre
siento girar la tierra

LIKE A SHIPWRECK

Like a shipwreck
a televised series
a program watched again and again
like a chair
like a dog at midnight
as if you were stripping me of my skin
and skin is infinite
we're alone
arms nails emptiness
to die I'd throw myself into the sea
to die I'd throw myself into the air
I'd cover myself fully
in dense and dark earth
I wouldn't be able to die
I'm not here no
I walk in the shadows of another life
I hang from the anvils and scaffolding
I become fire vegetation iron
sometimes I get up at dawn
to listen to the sirens of their voice
their proletarian day
goodbye thanks to the body
thanks to the gaze
only the strike the foam
only nakedness comforts me
I'm the earth and I undo myself
I come in through the windows
I call upon the doors of the houses
I watch the blood run
and feel the earth turn

con sus celdas sus manicomios
sus jefes de oficina
flotan pólizas de seguro
cartas donde una mujer abandona a su marido
hojas ángeles
los diarios denuncian la sedición
los focos comprobados
veo un hombre asesinado:
está llorando
su sangre está cubierta de moscas
su sangre torturada se levanta
y llena las paredes de rosas.

with its jail cells its mental hospitals
its office managers
insurance policies are floating
letters where wives abandon husbands
papers angels
the newspapers denounce sedition
the centers of protest are confirmed
I see a murdered man:
he's crying
his blood is covered in flies
his tortured blood rises up
and fills the walls with roses.

VIVIR MORIR ASÍ

Vivir morir así
profunda piedra
de sol de abrazos fieros
la luz rotunda
donde flotan los cuerpos
donde te hablo muerta
hay un caballo lejos
que espera en el silencio
sentirse en tanta muerte
saberse en tanta herida
sobre los pies pensando
me golpean me duelen
amor mío entonces descubro que eres tú
el mismo de la calle
que amanece
como la noche alada
siempre frente a mi puerta
porque nací en secreto
porque vivo en secreto
puedo volver al mar
ver a mi madre muerta
mirándome
abriendo un ojo inmenso
dulce petrificado.

TO LIVE AND DIE THIS WAY

To live and die this way
profound stone
of sun of fierce embraces
the total light
where the bodies float
where I speak to you while dead
far away there's a horse
who waits in the silence
to feel oneself in such death
to find oneself with such wounds
thinking on their feet
they're hitting me they're hurting me
and so my love I realize it's you
the same one from the street
that wakes up
like the winged night
constantly facing my door
because I was born in secret
because I live in secret
I can go back to the sea
see my dead mother
watching me
opening one sweet petrified
immense eye.

AIRE MÍO HOMBRE

Aire mío hombre
en tu cabeza toco mundos y seres
caminas sin saber que no eres tú
y pareces de pronto
una isla infinita
un verde trigo
una ciudad en donde
temerosas desvalidas prostitutas
llaman y se hunden para siempre
hay estadísticas hasta para las manos
tiene estado civil la muerte
por qué la furia
porque no nos iremos de este suelo
siempre cayendo con abrazos fusiles
entre gritos sirenas
sobrevolando cementerios aldeas
no sabíamos qué guerra
qué parto desde adentro
qué amanecer qué llaga
querido mío camarada
oh vivir siempre así como vivimos
atrás los cadáveres y los cedulones
todo lo que durante días y noches fuimos
las muertes
los delirios
ya no tengo memoria sino para mañana
me desentiendo de mí misma
y surjo y soy el desconocido
el hombre que va a morir
descubro ahora como en medio de un naufragio

MAN MY AIR

Man my air
in your head I touch worlds and beings
you walk without knowing you're not yourself
and suddenly you seem
like an infinite island
green wheat
a city in which
terrified helpless prostitutes
cry out and forever drown
there are statistics for everything even our hands
death has a civil status
why such rage
because we won't leave this place
we keep ending up with embraces rifles
among shouts sirens
flying over cemeteries villages
we didn't know what war
what birth pangs from within
what dawn what wound
my beloved comrade
oh to live always the way we do
behind corpses and unsettled accounts
all that we were for days and nights
the deaths
the delirium
I have barely enough memory for tomorrow
I can't handle myself
and I appear and I'm the stranger
the man who's going to die
as if in a shipwreck I now come to know

la hermosura de la muerte
el encuentro feroz con otras almas
libérame arrójame
siento el acero el hombre
el crujir de la noche asesinada por el miedo.

the beauty of death
the ferocious encounter with other souls
free me throw me
I feel the sword the man
the gnashing of a night murdered by fear.

HOY BESARÍA A LA GENTE DESCONOCIDA

Hoy besaría a la gente desconocida
y les pediría que vinieran a mí
porque sin ellos nada soy
de sus ojos inocentes terribles
está llena mi alma
ellos saben que nunca vendrán por mi esqueleto
porque quiero abrazarlos y no puedo
la última masacre sucedió entre mis uñas
esa gente que se cruza al camino
y nunca más
vive en mi lecho respira con mi sangre
por ellos soy
anónimo desconocido amor
qué bien hueles bajo las raíces
en la calle sobre los cementerios profundos
cómo te encuentro cuando
apuñalada entera me entrego
al sueño al hombre a la desdicha.

TODAY I'D KISS STRANGERS

Today I'd kiss strangers
and ask them to come to me
because I'm nothing without them
my soul is filled
with their innocent terrible eyes
they know they'll never come for my skeleton
because I yearn to embrace them and can't
the last massacre occurred between my nails
those people who cross the road
and then never again
they live in my bed they breathe with my blood
I live because of them
anonymous love of the stranger
how nice you smell under the roots
in the street over the deep cemeteries
this is how I find you when
completely stabbed I give myself over
to sleep to man to misfortune.

NO ME ALCANZAN LOS BRAZOS DE LA TIERRA

No me alcanzan los brazos de la tierra
no me alcanza la vida
mis amantes me duelen
andan por mi cerebro y son
la vida que no tuve
el silencio anterior
ya estoy definitiva muerta
tuve una casa
tuve tantos hijos subterráneos fantasmas
de noche me hostigaban
cosas y voces que no sé
tú podrías haber sido mi padre
tú podrías haber sido mi hijo
las calles por donde nos moríamos
no tenían sentido
despierta así no volverás a ser
tócame no hay parte de mi cuerpo
que no sea universal
sé que palpo en silencio
cosas que no he vivido
tristes constelaciones
piernas playas arenas
mutilados enfermos
yo nunca estaré muerta
me dolerán las uñas
los cuerpos los abrazos
los viajes
la aventura feroz de cada célula.

THE ARMS OF THE EARTH CAN'T HOLD ME

The arms of the earth can't hold me
life can't hold me
my lovers pain me
they walk through my brain and become
the life I never had
the previous silence
I'm now definitively dead
I had a house
I had so many underground ghost children
at night strange things unknown voices
would harass me
you could have been my father
you could have been my son
the streets where we died
made no sense
wake up and you won't live again
touch me there's no part of my body
that isn't universal
I know I touch in silence
things I've not experienced
sad constellations
legs beaches sands
the mutilated the infirm
I will never be dead
my nails will hurt
the bodies the embraces
the journeys
each cell's fierce adventure.

VÁMONOS HASTA LA HOJA VERDE

Vámonos hasta la hoja verde
vámonos al rocío
porque la muerte es larga
yo la he visto arrastrarse dorada
en la penumbra de las piezas
en los ojos amados
la he visto estrangulando
con pinceles y gasas
una noche en un grito de hospital
llegaron ángeles
vomitó la furia su esqueleto
espera
hay momentos para las manos
y las bocas vivas
rompe todos los mitos los teléfonos
los vientres se alucinan
de nosotros nacen seres oscuros
hombres taciturnos
tendrán tus ojos
hablarán con tu lengua
pasos mueven el mundo
este duro planeta que habitamos
irrumpe en este instante
soy inmortal y absurda cuando te siento
se demora la muerte
una noche otro día
alcanzan para hacernos saber que estamos vivos
tú plantas un rosal y la vida trasciende
del fondo de las bocas
nace un enjambre extraño

LET'S GO TO THE GREEN LEAF

Let's go to the green leaf
let's go to the dew
because death is long
I've seen it dragging itself golden
in the half-light of the rooms
in the beloved eyes
I've seen it strangling
with paintbrushes and gauze
one night angels arrived
to the sound of a hospital cry
the fury vomited her skeleton
wait
there are moments for hands
and living mouths
so break all the myths all the telephones
the wombs hallucinate
dark beings are born from us
taciturn men
will have your eyes
will speak with your tongue
footsteps move the world
this harsh planet we inhabit
barges in at this moment
I am immortal and absurd when I feel you
death is delayed
one night another day
are enough to let us know we're alive
you plant a rosebush and life spreads out
from the backs of mouths
a strange swarm of the saddest beings

de tristísimos seres
de pronto sobre los pies parados
diciendo amor noche desafío
de pronto tan inmensos
entregando la vida a un ojo ciego
a una sombra que mata
deja los dedos fríos
como la piedra amor
como el rocío.

is born
suddenly over the stilled feet
saying love night challenge
suddenly so immense
offering their life to a blind eye
a shadow that kills
and leaves fingers cold
like a stone my love
like the dew.

Y A FIN DE AÑO ES TRISTE

Y a fin de año es triste
y se avecina
todavía mis huesos mis ojos
todavía
crecen hijos puñales
anochece
30 de noviembre al despacho
la mañana está sola
la mañana
de la boca me nacen
plantas soles
de la boca henchida de tierra
muerte comprometida
vida comprometida
la mañana que cae
y es la mañana de un diciembre 1.

AND IT'S SAD AT THE END OF THE YEAR

And it's sad at the end of the year
and it's approaching
even now my bones my eyes
even now
children daggers grow
night falls
and sends November 30 away
the morning is lonely
the morning
plants suns
are born from my mouth
from my mouth swollen with soil
committed death
committed life
morning comes
the morning of some 1 December.

XVIII

De nuestros cuerpos haremos una sola casa
las estrellas bajan hasta los árboles
detienen el verano en mi cabeza
como en un dorado éxtasis
me dices hay un aire de otoño
y te asomas desnudo a la ventana
una gigantesca ausencia
se cierne sobre nosotros
y temblamos de vacío
todavía estoy viva
respiro aquí en la noche
aquí sola y asediada de enemigos
arriesgando todo destruyendo todo
he muerto
he invadido la noche tiernamente
con extensas poblaciones de estrellas
pero entiéndeme
ahora estoy hablando de morir contigo
de levantarme del lecho
buscándote en el silencio espectral
de convertirme en piedra de un río lejanísimo
debajo de mis pies
tus pies atónitos
yo fui una vez el aire que respiras
y si dices suicidio noche sueño
esto tan simple de estar vivo
es sólo una mentira
que nadie ha de creer.

XVIII

From our bodies we'll make a single house
the stars descend to the tree line
halting summer in my head
as if in a golden ecstasy
you say that autumn is in the air
and you lean out the window naked
a gigantic absence
hovers over us
and we tremble at the emptiness
I'm still alive
I breathe here at night
here alone and besieged by enemies
risking all destroying all
I have died
I have gently invaded the night
with vast populations of stars
but listen to me
right now I am speaking of dying with you
of getting out of bed
to seek you in the dim silence
I'm speaking of changing into a stone from a distant river
underneath my feet
your astounded feet
once I was the air you breathe
and if you say suicide night dream
this simple thing of being alive
it's only a lie
that no one should believe.

A Virginia

Quisiera vivir en África
en una selva de África
y que un inmenso león
me lamiera los pies
y me destrozara y me devorara
la frente qué estallido de nubes
el vientre qué pasaje de hormigas
los huesos tan feroces
volando de rama en rama un pájaro
así mi corazón que pesa tanto
podría dormirse en la montaña
quiero morir así
nunca en un lecho tibio
nunca entre paredes melodiosas
hay demasiada guerra en mí
para que pueda ceder
a la triste cordura de los anaqueles
basta de interrogatorios
quiero una hormiga un grito
de catástrofes se nutre mi esqueleto
hacia el secreto huyo
por golpes de teléfono
son las diez las diez de la mañana
ahora podría concebir un árbol
un hombre
darle por heredad todos mis ojos
mis uñas
eso que duele así
si yo viviera en África

To Virginia

I'd like to live in Africa
in a jungle in Africa
and I'd like an enormous lion
to lick my feet
rip me apart and devour me
what an explosion of clouds my forehead would be
and my womb what a path for ants
how ferocious my bones
a bird flying from branch to branch
in this way my heart that's so heavy
might fall asleep on the mountaintop
that's how I want to die
never in a lukewarm bed
never between melodious walls
there's too much of a fight in me
to let myself go
to the sad prudence of shelves
I'm sick of interrogations
I desire an ant a shout
of catastrophes nourishing my skeleton
I flee toward the secret
among the telephone's strikes
it's ten o'clock ten in the morning
right now I could conceive a tree
a man
give him all my eyes as an inheritance
my nails
everything that hurts like this
if I lived in Africa

en una selva de África
fuera tigre pantera o elefante
oh qué deseo de animalidad
qué río que arrebata
hambre de muerte y lunas
de puñales
oh desasida carne en fiera convertida
por fin segura y libre
cierta como la garra.

in a jungle in Africa
if I were a tiger a panther an elephant
what yearning for animality
what raging river
what hunger for death and moons
for daggers
oh ripped flesh transformed into fury
at last safe and free
as certain as a lion's claws.

EL OTOÑO ADELANTA

El otoño adelanta la desnudez del árbol
y la pobreza anuncia los huesos liberados
el origen violento
el descarnado soplo
te acostumbra
te viste de penumbras
de tazas derrumbadas
con las manos alcanza
zapatos para los pies remotos
somos pobres amor
somos la tierra profunda y desolada
abrazamos la noche
yo quiero esta pobreza
no ser no poseer nada
con ojos y con bocas macilentas y agrias
andar y ser el mundo
la cuchara.

AUTUMN HASTENS

Autumn hastens the nakedness of the tree
and poverty announces freed bones
the violent origin
the grim gust of wind
grooms you
dresses you in shadows
in shattered cups
with its hands it reaches
shoes for distant feet
we are poor my love
we are deep and desolate land
we embrace the night
I desire this poverty
not to be not to possess anything
with gaunt and sour eyes and mouths
to move and be the world
the spoon.

A Rosalía

Casi sin darnos cuenta
toda la primavera
Rosalía
como la luz y el aire
que no saben
viviéndote el rocío
el claro amanecer en que sonríes
vuelve con las ventanas de la vida
con el pan los quehaceres
deshojas calendarios para asomarte así
al día verdadero
al musical secreto de la rama
niña mujer espiga
lumbre de mis entrañas
rostro que verá el tiempo que yo quiero
el hombre que yo sueño
vuela
hoja del aire vuela
alondra de las siete vuela
por desatarse y ser
hay prisa en las entrañas de las cosas.

To Rosalía

Almost without noticing
all spring long
Rosalía
like light and air
that don't know
living your dew
the clear dawn when you smile
returns with the windows of life
with bread with chores
you tear pages from calendars to show yourself
to the true day
to the branch's musical secret
girl woman sprout
fire of my insides
face that will see the time I desire
the man I dream of
fly
fly leaf of air
fly seven a.m. lark
untie yourself and be
there is haste in the insides of things.

XXII

La noche es una pieza para siempre
una camisa clara
somos la noche amor
la noche elemental como la muerte
siento tu cuerpo siento
un herido de bala
un portafolio negro
un mar en la garganta
este cuarto nos mira desde adentro
exhausto de quehaceres zapatos cortinados
yo no sé por qué será la ropa
tan triste y tan profunda
yo no sé nada
ni siquiera he aprendido
cómo abrir una puerta
voy por el cuarto como por el aire
las ventanas combaten
las espaldas combaten
todo acecha es violencia
todo nos amenaza
el cuarto crea un jardín
un pozo de gemidos de voces de señales
oigo tus pensamientos
como un enorme río
como un gran abandono
siento en tu cuerpo el mundo
las sirenas el pánico
las playas desoladas
los perros callejeros
seres muertos que he amado.

XXII

The night is forever a room
a bright shirt
we are the night my love
the night as fundamental as death
I feel your body I feel
someone wounded by a bullet
a black briefcase
a sea in your throat
this room is watching us from inside
exhausted from chores shoes curtains
I don't know why clothes are
so sad and profound
I don't know anything
I haven't even learned
how to open a door
I move through the room as through air
the windows fight
the backs fight
everything stalks us it's violence
everything threatens us
the room creates a garden
a well of whimpers of voices of signs
I hear your thoughts
like an enormous river
like a great abandonment
I feel the world in your body
the sirens the panic
the desolate beaches
the stray dogs
dead beings I have loved.

DOS POEMAS A MAURICIO

I

He aquí las cartas que escribí
toda la tinta derramada en mi pecho
porque no estoy de noche
porque no estás conmigo hijo
y hay cosas que aún importan
porque no estás
llena de tus cuadernos
con tus ojos mis ojos
todos los ojos de los seres
de los árboles
efímeros felices
si voy por la calle y te llamo
y me miras distinto
porque no estoy
porque me he muerto en una esquina
yo te llamo te reclamo
secretamente
como la tierra reclama la lluvia
te llamo con un aullido verde
y tú te alejas
niño de la una de la mañana
inédito sin nombre sin sangre
siento en mi boca siento tu boca desvalida
tu estallido atómico
de todo esto sólo es cierto que he amado
y cuando me veas muerta no lo creas
porque muchos amores nacerán de mi muerte.

TWO POEMS FOR MAURICIO

I

Here are the letters I wrote
all the ink spilled on my chest
because I'm not here at night
because you're not with me son
and there are things that still matter
because you're not here
I'm filled with your notebooks
with your eyes my eyes
all the eyes of the beings
of the trees
ephemeral happy
if I go through the streets and call you
and you look at me differently
because I'm not here
because I've died on a street corner
I call you I claim you
secretly
like the earth claims the rain
I call out to you with a green howl
and you distance yourself
you 1 a.m. child
unpublished nameless bloodless
in my mouth I feel it I feel your mouth defenseless
your atomic crash
in all of this the only certainty is that I have loved
and when you see me dead don't believe it
because many loves will be born from my death.

II

Es mentira hijo que naciste de mí
de todas las mujeres y los hombres naciste
del dinosaurio oscuro
del petróleo
ascendiendo desde un cordón umbilical
flotando en el vacío
cosmonauta hombre-piedra
leñador huesos de mineral de hiedra
para perderte
para perderte siempre entre millones de formas
entre millones de hombres
huidizo niño del amanecer
igual que un golpe de madrugada
sobre un cadáver solo de madrugada
al que le digo que le amo y no despierta
al que le digo que le amo y no me abraza.

II

It's not true son that you were born of me
you were born of all women and all men
of the dark dinosaur
of petroleum
ascending from an umbilical cord
floating in the void
cosmonaut stone-man
woodcutter mineral ivy bones
to lose yourself
to lose yourself forever among millions of forms
among millions of men and women
elusive child of daybreak
on par with a strike of dawn
on a lone corpse of dawn
I say "I love you" and he doesn't wake up
I say "I love you" and he gives no hug.

AQUEL GOLPE ROTUNDO

Aquel golpe rotundo que sentiste
y que te despertó
2 de la madrugada
era yo
era mi corazón cavando un hoyo
rojo y desnudo como el sol.

THAT DECISIVE STRIKE

That decisive strike you felt
and that woke you up
2 in the morning
that was me
it was my heart digging a hole
red and naked as the sun.

Las ventanas segaron sus ingresos de luz
sus desafíos
adiós adiós
mi sangre
y el silencio
aquel silencio que solía dejarnos
más heridas y dulces
en las tardes de té
lo que me ha sucedido
y no lo sabes
con paredes deshechas
hombres mordiendo su locura
su vértigo
debió ser dulce entonces
dentro de tus entrañas
¡ay! detrás de tu lengua
de tus ojos
donde vivían abuelos y centauros
mares con corolas amarillas
y aladinos de fiebre
no sé morir en vano
sollozan sobre mí las madrugadas
tendedme sobre el mar
llevadme donde tu cuerpo
tu vientre me reclama
me está llamando madre
cuando amo es oscuro el cielo
y yo ando dentro tuyo
y todos los vestidos se quedan a la puerta
de la noche
qué raro era sentirte silenciosa
cuando mi cuerpo era otro cuerpo.

The windows reaped the benefits of light
the challenges
farewell farewell
my blood
and the silence
that silence that used to leave us
more wounds and sweets
at teatime
you don't even know
what has happened to me
with ruined walls
men biting their madness
their vertigo
it must have been sweet then
inside of you
oh! behind your tongue
your eyes
where grandparents and centaurs lived
seas with yellow corollas
and aladdins of fever
I don't know how to die in vain
the dawns sob over me
lay me down on the sea
take me to your body
your womb reclaims me
it's calling to me mother
when I love the sky is dark
and I dwell within you
and all the clothes are left at the door
of the night
how strange it was to feel you silent
when my body was another body.

TRANSLATOR'S NOTE

"Poetry lives in the void between words," said Selva Casal in an interview conducted by her fellow Uruguayan poet Silvia Guerra and published in the *Hispanic Poetry Review* in 2015. "The essence of my poetry can be found in something that colored my childhood, back when it was easy to climb the walls and hang from them like a tragic, most beautiful spider."

For this 90-year-old Uruguayan poet, writing is a daily affirmation of life, no matter what the season or state of the world. "I believe that even if there were no words, there would still be poetry. I really experience the poetry within daily life. For me each day is like the first day of Creation; I get up, look around, breathe—It's a privilege we don't always think about as we're drinking our coffee. To me it is very important."

There is something almost magical about poets who have lived and continued writing into their eighties or occasionally their nineties—their very age gives them a special authority. I remember as a teenager hearing a white-haired, wizard-like Stanley Kunitz read a poem about seeing Haley's Comet as a boy in 1910. He exuded an aura of joy, playfulness, and sheer delight at living. Around the same time, I traveled to Kraków to study Polish and had the privilege of hearing Nobel laureate Czesław Miłosz, then 91 years old, read his poems of witness to World War II and the oppressive era that followed it in Poland. Though laden with the weight of a painful history, Miłosz's reading also crackled with puns, jokes, and a sneaky sense of mischief.

This combination of intensity and playfulness was the same energy I felt when I first sat in Selva Casal's living room and leafed through her books while on a research trip to Uruguay in 2013. Reading her poems, which are simultaneously tragic and life-affirming with a clear-eyed view of the human condition, I knew I had to translate them. Of her sixteen books, I chose to translate this one in large part because Casal, who was living under a military dictatorship at the time of its publication, shared this writing at great personal risk and was prepared to face the consequences. For me, Casal stands in the company of Miłosz, Joseph Brodsky, Wisława Szymborska, Ernesto Cardenal, Juan Gelman, and so many other writers and artists from around the world who pierce through the rhetoric of tyrants. She's the kind of poet who reminds us why power-hungry rulers have always been wary of writers.

Born in 1930, Casal came from a highly educated family, and her father was also a poet. She worked as a penal lawyer and sociology professor while raising four children. Today she lives with her husband Arturo in an assisted living facility in Montevideo and continues to write every day. *No vivimos en vano* (Biblioteca Alfar, 1975) is her sixth book, published when she was 45 years old and living under a U.S.-backed military dictatorship that was illegally imprisoning, torturing, murdering, and disappearing thousands of people. Widely read as a denunciation of that dictatorship, the book resulted in Casal losing her teaching position at the Universidad de la República, a public university considered to be Uruguay's most important.

When I first started seeking to publish translations of Casal's poems in the U.S., I initially struggled. For some editors, poems written in response to late-twentieth-century dictatorships in Latin America might seem like ones we've heard before, familiar, even a cliché. Those comments frustrated me, as the history of repressive governments is one that many people in the U.S., such as my young university students, are unaware of. What is even more alarming is that they often do not know about their own country's long history of providing military and financial support to such governments—a reality that became common during the Cold War and continues in many parts of the world to this day. Unfortunately, the need to speak truth to power never goes away. It hardly seems coincidental that interest in Casal's work increased dramatically after 2016.

Today, I witness this book's publication amid a global pandemic, widespread political unrest, and an ongoing ecological crisis. In the U.S., it appears we may finally be starting to reckon with our "original sin" of racism, and this reckoning is echoing around the globe. Millions of people in our world continue to live in poverty and under the daily threat of violence. We could easily throw up our hands and say there is nothing we can do. But just the opposite is happening. Over the past months I've watched people go out of their way to deliver food to those most in need; I've seen people sew personal protective equipment for the most vulnerable; I've watched thousands take to the streets to stand up against racism and police brutality. "We do not live in vain," I hear them saying, all in their own language, their own cadence, their own voice.

In this attempt to carry Casal's message from the Spanish-speaking world of 1975 to the English-speaking one of 2020, I am seeking to transport her greatest poetic gifts: a keen insight into human nature, an awareness that goodness and evil are deeply intertwined within all human beings, and most important, a deep compassion for the Earth and all of its inhabitants. "Poetry has been my activism," said Casal in the 2015 interview with Silvia Guerra cited above. "It's my way of being in the world because indifference is corrosive. I couldn't separate myself from the things we've lived through in this country. Some of my poems touch upon this theme, which is like touching upon the drama of humanity itself."

For me, translation is always about so much more than words on a page. While I am devoted to the work, I often find myself falling in love with the poets themselves. This has never been truer with anyone than with Selva Casal. In a very personal way I admire her firm convictions, her resolution to keep writing well into old age, her generosity, and the playful sense of humor that poses a delightful contrast to the gravitas present in so much of her work.

Practically as soon as we met, I felt the urge to "adopt" her as a third grandmother, or perhaps more accurately, to be adopted by her. Like my own grandmothers, Casal welcomed me into her home with a smile, a hug, and a slice of cake. Like my own grandmothers, she told me powerful stories from the past. And, also like them, she gave me an example I feel compelled to follow—not just as a writer, but as a human being.

ACKNOWLEDGMENTS

First and foremost, I am grateful to Selva Casal herself for writing these poems, inviting me to translate them, and assisting me in the process with great warmth and hospitality. I also thank her husband Arturo Eguren for offering welcome and their daughter Virginia Eguren Casal for facilitating communication and offering much practical help—both in person and across distance.

I thank editor Laura Cesarco Eglin, Kristal Acuña, Margarita Mejía, Miranda Smith, cover designer Silvana Ayala, and everyone at Veliz Books for believing in this project and committing to it in spite of the obstacles along the way. I am also grateful to Laura for her incisive editorial work.

I am very thankful to the readers who answered questions and provided feedback on various versions of these poems: Janet Hendrickson, Oscar Montagut, Romina Freschi, and Keith Edkins. I must also offer special thanks to Martha Bátiz, Jesse Lee Kercheval, Seth Michelson, Michelle Gil-Montero, Indran Amirthanayagam, Rhonda Miska, and Ramiro Armas for accompanying and encouraging me in this project.

I thank my dear friends Wacław and Erdmute Sobaszek of Teatr Węgajty in Poland for offering their special tree as the book's cover image, and I thank Kaja Kwaśniewska for taking the picture.

I thank my colleagues and students at the University of Dubuque as well as my family and friends for their constant support.

Some of the poems in this volume (or versions of them) have appeared in the following publications: *Propeller Magazine*, *Waxwing*, *Presence: A Journal of Catholic Poetry*, *Shenandoah Review*, and *Spoon River Poetry Review*.

ABOUT THE POET

Selva Casal (born in 1930) lives in Montevideo, Uruguay and is the award-winning author of sixteen books of poetry, most recently *Abro las puertas de un jardín de plata* (I Open the Doors of a Silver Garden) (Trópico Sur Editor, 2014). A former penal lawyer, Casal is inspired by her experiences working with people who have faced injustice. Her 1975 publication of *No vivimos en vano* (*We Do Not Live in Vain*) during the military dictatorship in Uruguay resulted in her losing her position as a professor of sociology at Uruguay's Universidad de la República. Her work has received prizes in Uruguay, Argentina, and Mexico, such as the 2010 Premio Morosoli de Poesía given by the Fundación Lolita Rubial and the Premio Nacional del Ministerio de Educación y Cultura. Casal is also a painter and continues to write and paint daily. "Everything in life nourishes poetry," she says. "Everything."

ABOUT THE TRANSLATOR

Jeannine Marie Pitas is a Spanish-English translator, writer, and professor at the University of Dubuque, in Iowa. Her translation of Marosa di Giorgio's *I Remember Nightfall* (Ugly Duckling Presse, 2017) was shortlisted for the 2018 National Translation Award, and she contributed to the translation of Amanda Berenguer's *Materia Prima* (Ugly Duckling Presse, 2019), which was shortlisted for the 2020 Best Translated Book Award. She is the author of three poetry chapbooks and one full-length collection, *Things Seen and Unseen* (Mosaic Press, 2019). She is translation co-editor for *Presence: A Journal of Catholic Poetry*.